Nunavut

# Nunavut

Lyn Hancock

Lerner Publications Company

*This book is available in two editions:*
Library binding by Lerner Publications Company
Soft cover by First Avenue Editions, 1997.
241 First Avenue North
Minneapolis, MN 55401
ISBN: 0–8225–2758–8 (lib. bdg.)
ISBN: 0–8225–9800–0 (pbk.)

Website address: www.lernerbooks.com

LIBRARY OF CONGRESS
CATALOGING-IN-PUBLICATION DATA

Hancock, Lyn.
    Nunavut / by Lyn Hancock.
        p. cm. — (Hello Canada)
    Includes index.
    ISBN 0–8225–2758–8 (lib. bdg.)
    1. Inuit—Social life and customs—Juvenile literature.
    2. Nunavut (N.W.T.)—History—Juvenile literature.
    3. Nunavut (N.W.T.)—Social life and customs—Juvenile
    literature. [1. Nunavut (N.W.T.) 2. Inuit. 3. Eskimos.]
    I. Title. II. Series.
    E99.E9H35 1995
    971.9'2—dc20                                  94-33941

Manufactured in the United States of America
2 3 4 5 6 7 – JR – 02 01 00 99 98 97

Cover photograph by Lyn
Hancock.

The glossary that starts on page
72 gives definitions of words
shown in **bold type** in the text.

**Senior Editor**
Gretchen Bratvold
**Editor**
Domenica Di Piazza
**Photo Researcher**
Cindy Hartmon
**Series Designer**
Steve Foley
**Designer**
Darren Erickson

*Dedicated to my husband,
Frank Schober. We met in
Nunavut.*

 This book is printed on
acid-free, recyclable paper.

# Contents

# *Fun Facts*

🍁 Baker Lake in southern Nunavut is the geographic center of Canada. For this reason, the site is known as the Belly Button of Canada.

🍁 Trees do not grow in Nunavut. But in 1985, frozen fossils of ancient tree stumps were discovered on Axel Heiberg Island in northern Nunavut. The wood of the 45-million-year-old trees, which probably once stood 150 feet (46 meters) tall, was so well preserved that it could be sawed, split, and burned.

🍁 Because so few roads exist in Nunavut, residents of the territory travel by airplane five times more often than most other Canadians.

Hi! My name is Scooter. As you read *Nunavut,* I will be helping you make sense of some of the maps and charts that appear in the book.

**Inukshuk** *is an Inuit word for a pile of stones used as a landmark.*

🍁 Nunavut is shaped something like an *inukshuk,* or a pile of stones stacked to look like a human. An ancient form of communication, inukshuks were built to guide people across Arctic regions such as Nunavut, which has few natural landmarks.

🍁 The Aboriginal, or Native, people of Nunavut were once known as Eskimos, which means "eaters of raw meat" in the Algonquian Indian language. But the Native people in Nunavut call themselves Inuit, which simply means "the people."

7

*Only hardy flowers such as fireweed* (inset) *can grow in Nunavut, a land of mountains* (above) *and ice and snow* (facing page).

# *Above the Tree Line*

July 9, 1993, was an exciting day for the people who live at the top of the world. It was the birthday of Nunavut—a unique territory carved from Canada's Northwest Territories and a new name on the world map.

Most of Nunavut's inhabitants are Inuit. They named the territory Nunavut because in their language, Inuktitut, Nunavut means "our land." Inuit say their land is beautiful although it is buried under ice and snow. Even the sea is frozen. Sometimes it's hard to tell where the land ends and the sea begins.

Nunavut makes up one-fifth of Canada's land area. And with its many islands, bays, and channels, Nunavut has two-thirds of the country's coastline. Nunavut is larger than any other territory or province in Canada and is four times as big as the U.S. state of Texas.

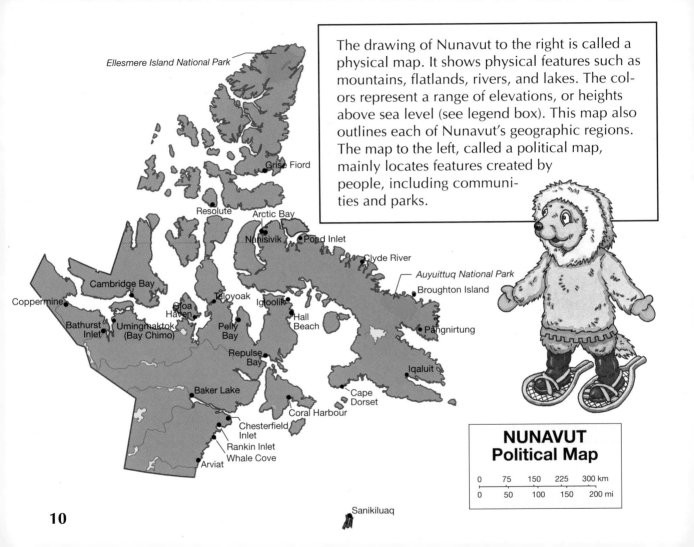

The drawing of Nunavut to the right is called a physical map. It shows physical features such as mountains, flatlands, rivers, and lakes. The colors represent a range of elevations, or heights above sea level (see legend box). This map also outlines each of Nunavut's geographic regions. The map to the left, called a political map, mainly locates features created by people, including communities and parks.

Ellesmere Island National Park

Grise Fiord

Resolute

Arctic Bay

Nanisivik    Pond Inlet

Clyde River

Auyuittuq National Park

Cambridge Bay

Coppermine

Taloyoak

Igloolik

Broughton Island

Gjoa Haven

Hall Beach

Bathurst Inlet

Umingmaktok (Bay Chimo)

Pelly Bay

Pangnirtung

Repulse Bay

Iqaluit

Baker Lake

Cape Dorset

Coral Harbour

Chesterfield Inlet

Rankin Inlet

Whale Cove

Arviat

Sanikiluaq

**NUNAVUT Political Map**

| 0 | 75 | 150 | 225 | 300 km |

| 0 | 50 | 100 | 150 | 200 mi |

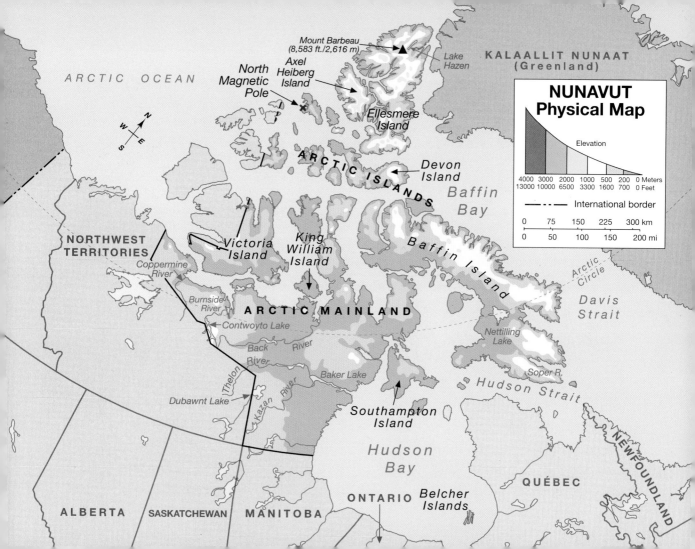

ARCTIC OCEAN

KALAALLIT NUNAAT
(Greenland)

Mount Barbeau
(8,583 ft./2,616 m)

Lake
Hazen

North
Magnetic
Pole

Axel
Heiberg
Island

Ellesmere
Island

N
W        E
S

ARCTIC ISLANDS

Devon
Island

Baffin
Bay

NUNAVUT
Physical Map

Elevation

| 4000 | 3000 | 2000 | 1000 | 500 | 200 | 0 Meters |
| 13000 | 10000 | 6500 | 3300 | 1600 | 700 | 0 Feet |

International border

| 0 | 75 | 150 | 225 | 300 km |
| 0 | 50 | 100 | 150 | 200 mi |

NORTHWEST
TERRITORIES

Victoria
Island

King
William
Island

Baffin Island

Arctic
Circle

Coppermine
River

Davis
Strait

Burnside
River

Contwoyto Lake

ARCTIC MAINLAND

Nettilling
Lake

Back        River
River

Soper R.

Baker Lake

Thelon

Dubawnt Lake

Kazan    River

Southampton
Island

Hudson Strait

Hudson
Bay

NEWFOUNDLAND

ALBERTA    SASKATCHEWAN    MANITOBA

ONTARIO    Belcher
Islands

QUÉBEC

*Coastal communities such as Hall Beach stretch along the waterfront.*

Nunavut's western neighbor is the Northwest Territories. To the east, across Baffin Bay and Davis Strait, lies Kalaallit Nunaat (Greenland), a huge island that belongs to the country of Denmark. Across the Arctic Ocean to the north, and on the other side of the frozen North Pole, is Russia.

The Canadian province of Manitoba borders Nunavut on the south. A large inland sea called Hudson Bay separates Nunavut from the province of Ontario. Across Hudson Strait, to the southeast of Nunavut, are the tips of two other Canadian provinces—Québec and Newfoundland.

*The Canadian Shield holds valuable minerals such as gold, nickel, zinc, copper, and iron ore.*

On a map, Nunavut's southern border lies along a line called the 60th parallel of latitude. That's why people in Nunavut say they live "North of 60" and call themselves northerners. They call anyone who lives "South of 60" a southerner. People in the territory also say they live "above the tree line" because they inhabit a region of the world where no trees grow.

Much of Nunavut rests on a vast foundation of hard rock called the Canadian Shield. Formed billions of years ago, the shield contains some of the oldest rocks in the world. In some parts of Nunavut, the shield is covered by younger rocks and plants. In other places, the original rock lies naked for all to see.

*Thousands of glaciers remain in some areas of the Arctic Islands.*

During the last **Ice Age,** which ended about 10,000 years ago, huge masses of ice up to three miles (five kilometers) thick moved across what is now Nunavut. Called **glaciers,** these sheets of ice stripped the land, shattered and polished the rocks, and gouged out large hollows that later filled with water to form lakes. When the glaciers eventually melted, they left behind the rugged landscape that makes up Nunavut.

Nunavut is divided into two main land regions—the Arctic Mainland and the Arctic Islands. On a map, the islands look something like a huge jigsaw puzzle. The largest include Baffin, Ellesmere, and Victoria Islands. High, ice-capped mountains rise on the northern and eastern islands. Reaching 8,583 feet (2,616 m), Mount Barbeau on Ellesmere Island is the highest peak in Nunavut.

The remaining Arctic Islands, as well as the Arctic Mainland, are flat and rocky. Here and there, low hills and snaking gravel ridges called **eskers** break the flat plain. So do **swamps** (a type of wetland), countless lakes, and long, winding rivers.

Among Nunavut's many waterways are the Coppermine and the Back Rivers, which head north to the Arctic Ocean. The Thelon and the Kazan flow east into Hudson Bay. Some of the biggest lakes include Nettilling Lake on Baffin Island and Dubawnt Lake on the Arctic Mainland. So many smaller lakes dot Nunavut that most have not been named.

*Wilberforce Falls on the Hood River is the highest waterfall north of the Arctic Circle, a line that marks the southern boundary of the Arctic on the globe.*

*A community on Baffin Island is nestled at the foot of mountains.*

North of 60, communities are small, few in number, and far away from one another. Major centers include the coastal communities of Iqaluit, Rankin Inlet, and Cambridge Bay. Adventurers heading for the North Pole often start the trip in Resolute on Cornwallis Island. Tourists visit Pangnirtung on Baffin Island to enjoy the mountain scenery. Grise Fiord is Nunavut's northernmost community.

Nunavut has the coldest weather in Canada. The average summer temperature is only 48° F (9° C). During winter, which lasts about nine months, the average temperature dips to an icy –22° F (–30° C). Chilling winds, blizzards, and blowing snow make the winters seem even colder.

On the other hand, some areas in Nunavut can get quite warm. On July

15, 1989, the coastal community of Coppermine in western Nunavut recorded the highest temperature in Canada for that day—93° F (34° C) in the shade!

Nunavut is sometimes called Land of the Midnight Sun. This is because during summer, the North Pole tilts toward the sun. As a result, the areas of Nunavut that are closest to the North Pole have summer days of almost continual sunlight—even at midnight! The opposite is true in winter, when the North Pole tilts away from the sun. During much of this time, the northernmost parts of the territory experience almost constant darkness.

The amount of **precipitation** (rain and snow) in Nunavut varies. Some parts of the Arctic Islands get so little precipitation that they are dry enough to be called **deserts.** Parts of Ellesmere Island, for example, receive only 2.5 inches (6 centimeters) of rain and snow each year. As much as 39 inches (100 cm) may fall annually on other islands or on the mainland.

*The summer sky glows at midnight.*

*Chunks of ice* (facing page) **break off glaciers that are close to the sea, forming icebergs. On land, colorful saxifrage** (inset top), ***arctic poppies*** (inset center), ***and berries*** (inset bottom and top right) **thrive in summer even though the ground below is still frozen** (above).

Because temperatures in Nunavut remain below 32° F (0° C) for long periods of time, most of the soil is per- manently frozen. Called **permafrost,** this ground is frozen in some places to a depth of several hundred feet.

Nunavut's frozen, treeless landscape is known as **tundra.** When summer arrives, a thin layer of surface soil thaws and plants can grow, with help from long, sunny days and water from melt- ing snow. Although summer may be as short as six weeks in some areas of Nunavut, lichens, mosses, grasses, ber- ries, shrubs, and flowers thrive.

These tundra plants have adapted, or changed, to survive in the territory's harsh, Arctic climate. Arctic poppies and mountain avens, for example, ro- tate their petals so that they face the sun all day long. Low-growing shrubs, such as arctic willows and dwarf birches, spread their branches along the ground to avoid the drying wind.

Few kinds of wildlife live in Nunavut. But the territory's animals are very important to the Inuit, who rely on them for food and clothing. The Inuit also carve artworks from animal materials such as caribou antlers and whalebone. Living on the land (away from settlements) and hunting for birds, fish, and mammals is an important part of Inuit culture.

Polar bears and arctic foxes, for example, are valued for their fur. Whales such as belugas and narwhals are prized for their muktuk, a layer of skin and blubber that Inuit eat like candy. Woolly musk oxen, which look as if they just stepped out of the Ice Age, are hunted for their meat and wool. The meat of the barren-ground caribou is the most important food of all.

Only a few kinds of birds—including ravens, snowy owls, and gyrfalcons—spend the entire year in Nunavut. Millions of other birds, such as arctic terns and golden plovers, fly north each spring to raise their young. Seabirds such as murres, fulmars, and kittiwakes nest by the thousands on Nunavut's high cliffs and rocky islands.

*Male polar bears* (above) *and musk oxen* (center) *can weigh almost 1,000 pounds (454 kilograms). Young people admire newly hatched snowy owls* (right). *The baby birds will one day grow to 20 inches (51 centimeters) in length* (far right).

21

# Aboriginals and Newcomers

No one knows for sure when people first came to what is now Nunavut. Many experts believe that distant ancestors of the Inuit made their way to North America about 10,000 years ago, by crossing the Bering Strait from Asia into what is now Alaska. About 6,000 years later, descendants of these people traveled from Alaska eastward to the Canadian Arctic.

Known as Pre-Dorset people, the travelers journeyed on foot, seeking game animals such as seals, walrus, and caribou. The hunters killed their prey with weapons crafted from stones, antlers, and bones. Tents made from animal hides provided shelter. When the hunters were ready to move on, they piled their gear onto sleds and pulled them to new hunting grounds.

# The First Inuit

The Inuit have many traditional tales that explain the world around them. One story tells of the creation of the world's first people. According to this tale, a girl married a dog. Her father sent the pair off to a small, rocky island, where the girl gave birth to many children, some dog-children and some human. To get food, the children's dog-father would swim

across the water wearing a pair of boots around his neck, and the girl's father would put meat in the boots. One day the girl's father put heavy rocks under the meat, and the dog drowned.

Angry at her father, the girl told her children to attack their grandfather and eat him up, which they did. But without the grandfather, the children had no food. So the girl sent one group of children inland to live on caribou. This group became the first Indians. The second group she sent to the east, telling them to plant their food in the ground. These became the first white people. The girl sent the rest of her children to the north and told them that there wouldn't be much food there, so they should take whatever they could find. These children became the first Inuit.

The descendants of the Pre-Dorsets were also hunters. Called the Dorset people, they lived during the summer in hide tents. In winter some Dorset groups built snowhouses—rounded shelters crafted from snow and blocks of ice. Other groups dug rectangular, underground dwellings. To heat and light their homes, the Dorset people invented a lamp made from a soft stone called soapstone. Fueled by seal oil, the flames of the lamps were also used for cooking.

The first Europeans to visit what is now Nunavut were Norse explorers. They sailed to Baffin Island from Greenland in about A.D. 1000 but made no settlements there.

At about the same time, groups of Native people known as the Thule moved east from Alaska to the Arctic Islands. They copied the Dorsets' idea of building snowhouses, which the Thule people used as temporary shelters when hunting or when gathering to sing, dance, and tell stories.

Most of the year, the Thule lived in small coastal villages. Their round homes were built partly underground for warmth. Each house had floors and walls of stone, a whalebone frame, and a sealskin roof covered with sod (blocks of earth and grass). In summer the Thule lived in skin tents.

The Thule were experts at harpooning whales. Sometimes they hunted these large sea mammals from narrow, sealskin-covered boats known as kayaks. Other times the hunters rode in umiaks—big, open boats used primarily to carry families and their belongings from camp to camp.

To keep water out of kayaks (above), *hunters have for centuries tied their waterproof parkas around the rim of the opening in which they sit. A dwelling* (left) *discovered on an island in the Burnside River is thought to be almost 600 years old. The roof was built from caribou antlers.*

Starting in the 1600s, the Arctic climate gradually grew colder. Whales left their usual travel routes, probably to find warmer waters. With fewer whales to hunt, people hunted seals and walrus. Some Thule abandoned their coastal villages and moved inland, where they tracked caribou. These were the beginnings of Inuit culture.

Like their ancestors, Inuit followed animals according to the seasons. In spring the people caught fish and birds and harpooned seals and walrus at the edge of the frozen sea. In summer and

**Inuit relied on seals** (above) **and fish** (right) **for food.**

fall, Inuit went inland to hunt caribou and musk oxen with spears and arrows. They gathered berries and trapped fish in underwater stone fences called weirs. In winter the people waited patiently on the ice to harpoon seals at breathing holes, where the sea animals came up for air. Inuit also hunted whales, which eventually returned to the Arctic after the climate warmed.

Hundreds of years after the Norse, other Europeans began to come to the region. In 1576 a British sea captain named Martin Frobisher landed on Baffin Island, which he claimed for England the next year.

Other explorers headed for the Arctic to find fur-bearing animals. In 1670 the British government gave a huge piece of land surrounding Hudson Bay to a fur-trading organization

*To build snowhouses, men and women cut and stacked blocks of hard snow to form a dome. Cracks between the blocks were tightly packed with snow to keep out harsh winds.*

called the Hudson's Bay Company. Britain called the entire region Rupert's Land. A small part of what is now Nunavut was included in this territory.

The fur trade did not expand into Nunavut until many years later, but Europeans continued to explore and map the region. Few of them, however, tried to learn from the Inuit how to live in the Arctic. As a result, many of the explorers suffered or died from cold, diseases, and starvation. But those who adopted the food and clothing of the Inuit usually survived.

Starting in the early 1800s, American and European whalers headed for what is now Nunavut to kill the huge bowhead whales that filled the waters off Baffin Island. Each whale was worth $100,000—an enormous amount of money at that time. Baleen, or whalebone, was used to stiffen women's corsets. Workers boiled whale blubber to make oil for fueling lamps and for manufacturing soap and paint.

## Frozen in Time

For hundreds of years, explorers traveled across what is now Nunavut looking for the Northwest Passage, a sea route from Europe to Asia by way of the Arctic Islands. One famous journey was led by John Franklin, a British sea captain. In 1845 he and his crew headed across Davis Strait to begin their search for the route. They were never heard from again.

More than 20 expeditions crisscrossed the Arctic looking for Franklin. From the discovery of Franklin's records, explorers learned that in 1846 Franklin's ships got stuck in sea ice off King William Island. A year and a half later, they were still stuck, and Franklin and 24 sailors had died. Another 104 crew members headed south across the frozen Arctic on foot, hoping to make it to a trading post hundreds of miles away. They never made it.

People wondered why so many of Franklin's sailors had died, even though the ships had plenty of food on board. They also wondered why the sailors who set off on foot had taken curtain rods and a desk instead of warm clothing for their trek across the Arctic.

The answers came in the mid-1980s, when scientists dug up the almost perfectly preserved frozen body of crew member John Torrington *(below)*. The scientists discovered that Torrington had high levels of lead in his body. From the remains of garbage left behind by Franklin's crew, the scientists learned that Torrington and the other crew members had eaten from tin cans sealed with lead, which seeped into the food and eventually caused lead poisoning. Large amounts of lead can cause brain damage and even death. Some of the deaths and the unwise and tragic decisions of the Franklin expedition may have been the result of too much lead.

Inuit guided the whalers across the region and provided them with food and clothing. Inuit soon came to depend on the money, guns, and cloth they received in exchange.

In 1867 the British **colonies,** or settlements, in what is now southeastern Canada formed a new country called the Dominion of Canada. Three years later, Canada bought Rupert's Land from the Hudson's Bay Company and gained control of the neighboring North-western Territory. The Canadian government then combined the two areas into the North-West Territories, which included all of what is now Nunavut.

By the end of the 1800s, most bowhead whales had been killed. European and American hunters in Nunavut began seeking smaller whales, such as

belugas and narwhals, which were more plentiful. Eventually most of these whales also were killed, and the area's whaling industry came to an end.

Some whalers left what is now Nunavut, but others stayed to open fur-trading posts. The Hudson's Bay Company also set up posts in what is now Nunavut and encouraged Inuit to hunt and trap animals for the firm. The Inuit traded arctic fox and polar bear furs, seal and walrus skins, narwhal tusks, and fresh meat for guns, metal tools, wooden boats, cotton cloth, flour, tea, sugar, and tobacco.

Whaling and trapping suited the Inuit lifestyle. But foreign whalers and traders brought new diseases that the Native people in what is now Nunavut had never been exposed to. With no natural resistance to these illnesses, entire communities died. Some groups, such as the Sallirmiut Inuit of Southampton Island, had all died by the end of the 1800s.

At about the same time, **missionaries** came to Nunavut to teach the Christian religion to the Inuit. In 1894 Reverend Edmund Peck set up the first permanent mission at the whaling station on Blacklead Island.

The missionaries built schools and hospitals. Peck developed a method of writing Inuktitut, the Inuit language. For each syllable (combination of sounds) in the language, Peck created a written symbol. Before this, Inuktitut had been a spoken language only.

But the missionaries caused problems, too. They persuaded Inuit families to send their children to schools far from home for years at a time. While learning new ways from the missionaries, many Inuit lost touch with their own beliefs and traditions.

*Missionaries such as Reverend Edmund Peck introduced writing to the Inuit.*

32

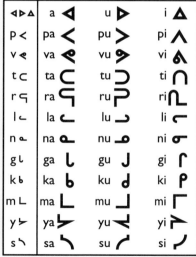

# How Do You Spell Nunavut?

The system of writing that missionaries introduced to the Inuit is called syllabic writing. In the Roman alphabet, used for writing English and many other languages, a letter stands for a particular sound. But in syllabic writing, each symbol stands for a syllable, or combination of sounds. The wall hanging above—made by students in Igloolik, Nunavut—shows how Nunavut is written in English *(right)* and in Inuktitut *(left),* the Inuit language.

# *From Mounties to the Birth of Nunavut*

Beginning in 1903, the Royal Canadian Mounted Police went North of 60 to set up police posts and to make regular patrols. Sent by the Canadian government, they traveled by boat and dog team. The Mounties visited whaling stations, trading posts, and Inuit camps. At each stop, the Mounties told both Natives and non-Natives that the land belonged to Canada and was called the North-West Territories. This meant that the people in the region had to obey Canadian laws.

The Canadian laws and procedures, however, did not allow Inuit to follow many of their traditions. And the laws sometimes conflicted with decisions made by missionaries in the area.

34

*In 1909 U.S. explorer Robert Peary* (facing page) *and two Inuit guides traveled by sled across the frozen Arctic Ocean, becoming among the first to reach the North Pole. A policeman* (right) *stands in front of a Royal Canadian Mounted Police station on Ellesmere Island.*

Inuit families, for example, gave their children only one name. Church leaders gave Inuit another name, either from the Bible or an English name that sounded something like the original Inuit name. The Canadian government, thinking that Native names were too complicated, assigned numbers to the Inuit. Eventually the government gave up the numbers and made Inuit add family names so that everyone would have two names.

More changes to Inuit life came after World War II started in 1939. Thousands of U. S. soldiers and construction workers from southern Canada arrived in the Northwest Territories to build airfields and other defense sites. Military planes were stationed at the airfields to defend North America if enemy planes from Japan or Germany attacked from over the North Pole.

After the war ended in 1945, the Soviet Union became a bitter enemy of the United States and Canada. In 1954 Canada and the United States agreed to build a chain of airfields and radar sites called the Distant Early Warning Line. Stretching from Alaska to Baffin Island, the line helped the two countries keep watch for any Soviet aircraft that might cross over the North Pole to drop their bombs.

This project offered steady jobs that provided Inuit with cash wages. As a result, many Inuit abandoned their hunting and trapping lifestyle and moved to areas where they could find paid jobs.

Wage jobs attracted Inuit because making a living from the land had become very difficult. Prices for furs were low at this time. Caribou herds had strayed from their usual routes and were more difficult to find. In addition, a disease called tuberculosis was widespread. Large numbers of Inuit died from the illness or from starvation.

*By 1957 Distant Early Warning Line radar stations* (above) *had been built in Nunavut. Most Inuit at that time lived on the land. Every so often, hunters went to trading posts* (right) *to exchange furs for tokens, which could be traded for goods.*

*The Canadian government encouraged Inuit to leave their camps and settle in communities built near trading posts.*

In the 1950s, the Canadian government decided to help the Inuit. The government persuaded many of the Native people to leave their camps and to move into permanent communities. There, officials provided food, education, money, and shelter. Workers built schools, houses, nursing stations, offices, and power plants. Later community halls, recreation centers, and airports were also constructed.

As a result, life became more comfortable for Aboriginal people in Nunavut. But with such big changes in their way of living, Inuit lost their independence. The priests, police, game wardens, nurses, social workers, and other professionals from southern Canada took over responsibilities that had once belonged to Inuit elders and leaders. Young Inuit who spoke English and were educated in the new ways also took over leadership positions.

Inuit elders, who had been highly respected in the old culture, now felt useless and rejected. Many Inuit were bored without the responsibilities that had kept them busy and had given them a sense of pride when they were living on the land.

So many changes in such a short time caused many Inuit to lose control of their lives. Some people drank too much alcohol, got into fights, or took drugs. Others committed suicide.

Despite these problems, Inuit remained strong. Having survived for thousands of years in the most difficult conditions on earth, they were used to finding practical ways to solve their problems. One of these ways has been to share and work together.

*An Inuit mother in Coppermine signs papers to receive money from the Canadian government to help pay her family's expenses. In settled communities away from the land, Inuit could no longer use traditional skills to meet all their needs.*

*A weaver in Pangnirtung works on a wall hanging.*

In the 1950s, Inuit communities started co-operatives, or co-ops, to create jobs and to encourage pride in Native culture. These organizations made and sold Native arts and crafts, ran hotels and fishing lodges, delivered water and fuel, and sold groceries. The co-ops, which still exist, share their profits with all of their members.

Inuit also joined with other Aboriginal groups to form development corporations. With help from non-Native advisers, these organizations have given Inuit experience in investing money and running businesses, such as airlines and construction companies.

To help Inuit gain more control over their lives, a group of young Inuit leaders started working in the 1970s to

*Inuit leader Paul Quassa* (left) *and Canada's prime minister, Brian Mulroney* (right), *talk at the May 25, 1993, signing of the agreement to create Nunavut.*

In 1982 the government of the Northwest Territories agreed to give residents a chance to vote on the idea. A majority of people voted to divide the region in two. Ten years later, in 1992, another election was held to decide the boundaries of the new territory. As a result of these elections, the Canadian government has agreed that the eastern Arctic region will become the territory of Nunavut. The western Arctic region will remain in the Northwest Territories.

create a new territory to be governed by Inuit. They suggested that the Northwest Territories be divided in two. The eastern part of the territory, where Inuit are a majority, would be called Nunavut.

**41**

*A crowd* (left) *cheers at the first celebration of Nunavut Day on July 9, 1993. Well-known Inuit artist Kenojuak Ashevak drew an illustration* (facing page) *to mark the creation of the new territory.*

The government of Nunavut will be in place by 1999. In the meantime, Inuit leaders are working with government officials to plan Nunavut's new government and to train Inuit to run it.

Everyone—Inuit and non-Inuit—over the age of 16 will be allowed to vote and to run for public office. Inuit traditions will be followed as much as possible. And the new territory will have three official languages—English, French, and Inuktitut. In the same way inukshuks guide travelers, the people of Nunavut can be guides for the rest of the world as they create their new system of government.

# Making a Living in Nunavut

Except for a few streets in each community and one short road on Baffin Island between the settlements of Arctic Bay and Nanisivik, Nunavut has no all-season roads. People travel along trails formed by game animals or on specially constructed winter roads made from ice and snow. For short trips, most people use a snowmobile in winter and an all-terrain vehicle in summer.

For longer journeys, people must fly. Some of Nunavut's residents take regularly scheduled flights to get from one community to another. Others charter, or rent, a plane. In Nunavut traveling by airplane is as common as taking the bus is in other parts of the world.

*People in Nunavut rely on many forms of transportation—including planes* (above) *and icebreakers* (below)—*to get around. A hiker* (inset) *stands near a sign that shows how far Nunavut is from other places on the globe.*

Besides transporting people, airplanes bring food and other goods to Nunavut, which has few factories and no farms. But flying is expensive. Items flown in by plane cost two or three times more in Nunavut than they do in southern Canada. Shipping by water is much cheaper—but much slower. Tugboats and barges carry heavy goods north by following the long Mackenzie River in the Northwest Territories or by crossing Hudson Bay. Then ice-breaking ships, which can plow through thick sea ice, take the goods to settlements along the Arctic coast.

Because Nunavut is so remote and transportation is either slow or expensive, few industries have developed in the territory. In addition, Nunavut's economy is shaped by how residents live. Most Inuit, for example, do not make their living from full-time jobs that pay wages, either because jobs are not available or because the people lack specific job skills. Instead most Inuit work at a bit of everything. When jobs are available, Inuit do seasonal work such as guiding tourists or constructing buildings. They fish and hunt caribou and musk oxen for food and clothing. In some cases, they earn extra money by selling some of the animals' meat.

Almost half of all Inuit households earn extra cash by making traditional artwork such as carvings from whale-bone, antlers, and stones. They also produce drawings, prints, and cloth-ing. Most artists work in their own homes and sell these highly prized items to local co-ops, which then sell the art to galleries throughout the world.

*Many Inuit families* (facing page, left) *rely on hunting and fishing for food. After a seal hunt, women scrape off the animal's skin* (facing page, right). *Fish often hang to dry* (above) *in the home.*

The symbols on this map show where different economic activities take place in Nunavut. The legend in the box to the upper right explains what each symbol stands for. Because the map is small, not every community's activities are represented. Government jobs and arts and crafts, for example, are in every community. Tourism is important throughout Nunavut, and mining exploration is growing quickly in many places.

## NUNAVUT Economic Map

- Mining
- Oil/Natural gas
- Tourism
- Manufacturing
- Weather station
- Government
- Boating
- Arts and crafts

On the other hand, almost all non-Inuit workers have permanent, wage-earning jobs in major centers such as Iqaluit, Rankin Inlet, and Cambridge Bay. Non-Inuit hold most of Nunavut's skilled jobs, which include teaching, nursing, and managing businesses.

About 87 percent of wage earners in Nunavut have service jobs helping people or businesses. Almost half of these service workers are employed by the government. Some people are politicians, administrators, consultants, or police officers. Other government service workers are teachers, nurses, doctors, engineers, mechanics, garbage collectors, electricians, or plumbers.

More than 400 service workers in Nunavut help tourists. In fact, tourism is the fastest growing part of the territory's economy. Inuit are being trained

*Pilots are among Nunavut's many service workers.*

for jobs as tour guides, hotel clerks, and cooks. Tourist workers also serve as outfitters—people who rent outdoor equipment such as tents and kayaks to visitors who come to explore Nunavut's unspoiled wilderness.

49

*A kayaker heads out to test his skills.*

Paddling wild rivers such as the Thelon or kayaking among the Arctic Islands are popular activities. Almost every community has hunting and fishing guides. People also hike across the tundra or climb mountains and glaciers in Ellesmere Island and Auyuittuq National Parks. Many outfitters arrange for visitors to stay with Inuit families or to watch Inuit artists at work.

**The Polaris zinc and lead mine** (above) **provides jobs for about 275 workers in Nunavut. Some other miners earn a living looking for diamonds** (inset).

Nunavut's birthrate, or the number of people born there each year, is twice as high as those in most other parts of Canada. For this reason, communities in the territory are growing rapidly, and construction is booming. About 6 percent of wage earners in Nunavut have construction jobs, building new schools, offices, community centers, and homes.

With rich deposits of minerals, Nunavut's mining industry employs about 4 percent of the territory's wage earners. Miners in Nunavut dig for lead and zinc at the Polaris mine on Little Cornwallis Island or at the Nanisivik mine near Arctic Bay. The Lupin mine on Contwoyto Lake is the world's northernmost gold mine outside of Russia. This mine in southwestern Nunavut is one of Canada's top five gold producers.

Oil and gas have been discovered in Nunavut, but only one small oil field—Bent Horn on Cameron Island—is in production. Each summer one or two tankerloads of oil from this field are shipped to a refinery in Québec, where the oil is processed.

# Canada's First Earth School

Only 260 children attend Joamie Ilin-niarvik School in Iqaluit, but they did 1,000 environmental awareness projects in only two years. As part of a Canadian competition in which thousands of other schools participated, the students at Joamie School were the first to complete this many projects.

Joamie kids have done a lot. They set up an environmental resource library, built nature trails, and prepared posters *(right)*, booklets, and activity kits on a variety of environmental topics. They also conducted community cleanups, recycled waste, and adopted a plot of land and

a pond to study and care for. Students at the school also made soil by collecting kitchen waste and waiting for it to rot and decay—a process called composting.

Students bring lunch to school in reusable containers, recycle their pop cans, and pride themselves on having almost garbage-free lunches. They also nudge their parents into being environmentally conscious. Young people remind adults to turn off lights, to find ways to recycle things, and to take shorter showers to conserve water. For all their efforts, Joamie students won their school the title Earth School.

Few factories exist in Nunavut. In fact, only 1 percent of the territory's wage earners have manufacturing jobs. Most factory workers process food for a living. These laborers cut up and package raw fish and meat. The products are then sold in Nunavut and in southern Canada. Inuit are being trained at a plant in Pangnirtung to catch and process turbot, shrimp, and scallops for sale to international markets. To create more jobs, Nunavut plans to build new factories, where workers will prepare smoked fish and dried meat.

Because Nunavut has few people, very little manufacturing, and no agriculture, the territory is one of the last places in the world where land, air, and water are relatively unspoiled. Almost all types of wildlife native to the

*Workers at a fish plant in Cambridge Bay fillet, or slice, arctic char.*

region still thrive. The people of Nunavut are determined to keep it that way.

Managing land and wildlife so that both are used wisely is a top priority in Nunavut. As a well-known saying goes, "We do not inherit the land and its resources from our ancestors. We borrow it from our children."

# *The Best of Two Worlds*

A fascinating mix of cultures exists in Nunavut. Inuit often wear baseball caps and bomber jackets. Non-Inuit wear parkas trimmed with fur and decorated with sewn-on images of polar bears. Inuit cartoons feature Super Shamou, a character modeled after world-famous Superman.

*Although commercial whaling is illegal worldwide, Inuit have traditionally relied on whales for food and are still allowed to hunt certain types of whales.*

A Christmas celebration in a small Nunavut community is another example of how Inuit and non-Inuit combine the best of two worlds. After church services, people of all ages crowd into the community hall to eat, dance, and play games. Baked turkey and apple pie are served beside raw seal and frozen fish. Ancient drum dances are followed by rock-and-roll music. Games include trying to open a well-wrapped gift while wearing heavy sealskin mitts.

Only 24,730 people live in Nunavut. Inuit make up 80 percent of the territory's population. The remaining 20 percent are mostly people of British and European descent. Nunavut's residents are scattered throughout the territory in 28 isolated communities. These centers may be as large as Iqaluit, which has 4,220 residents, or as small as

*Friends* (left) *sit atop a crate of building materials. Because the ground in Nunavut is permanently frozen, all buildings are constructed to sit completely above the ground. Even the pipes* (below) *carrying water, fuel, and waste must be above ground.*

Bathurst Inlet, with a population of 18. Some families choose to live on the land in outpost camps, away from settlements.

Great distances do not stop the people of Nunavut from coming together often to have fun. Celebrations, community feasts, sporting events, festivals, and concerts are popular activities. These shared events help Nunavut's Inuit and non-Inuit cultures understand one another.

People in Nunavut love sports. Popular non-Inuit games include hockey, curling, and badminton. Inuit games are played by only one or two people and require little equipment. Some of these games seem like torture to non-Inuit. In ear lift, contestants hang as much as 15 pounds (7 kilograms) of lead from their ears and carry this weight as far as possible.

**58**

*Inuit athletic events include arm wrestling* (facing page, left) *and pole twist* (facing page, right). *Even without smooth, grassy courses to play on, golf* (above) *is popular in Nunavut!*

Every two years, Nunavut's athletes join with those from Alaska, Greenland, and other Arctic countries for the Arctic Winter Games. People compete in cross-country skiing, indoor soccer, and figure skating. They also take part in the Inuit version of wrestling, in which contestants use only the strength of their arms and shoulders—not their legs —to pin their opponent to the floor.

Almost every community in Nunavut has a carnival to celebrate the arrival of spring—even though snow is usually still on the ground! The biggest spring carnival is Toonik Tyme in Iqaluit. The event starts with a parade and ends with a feast. In between, people enjoy building snowhouses and racing snowmobiles and dogsleds.

**59**

In summer people in Nunavut meet for a festival called Northern Games. Among the main activities at this event are the Good Woman and the Good Man contests, where men and women test some of the skills they need to care for a family in Nunavut. This includes boiling tea, plucking ducks, skinning seals, and making a flat bread called bannock.

Music is a big part of all celebrations in Nunavut. During many traditional events, people chant and dance to the beat of a drum. In throat singing, two or three women stand face to face with their mouths directly opposite the others' and make rhythmic noises with their throats. People do American square dances, Scottish reels, and Irish jigs to the music of fiddles and accordions. Inuit also enjoy dancing to rock music or doing line dances.

Respect for one another's culture also comes through drama. Actors at the Tunooniq Theatre in Pond Inlet put on plays to portray history and modern life from the Inuit point of view. The Inuit actors combine storytelling, drum dancing, and chanting.

*An actor from the Tunooniq Theatre wears traditional Inuit clothing and mukluks, or boots made from sealskin.*

*A group of square dancers* (above) *celebrate Nunavut Day. In traditional drumming* (right), *the drummer beats both sides of the instrument while chanting and swaying to the rhythm.*

Contact with non-Inuit long ago caused Inuit to lose parts of their culture. Nowadays non-Inuit and Inuit are working together to ensure that the old ways are remembered. More Inuit are training to be teachers. Schools invite Inuit elders into classrooms to share knowledge. Some classes are taught in Inuktitut. And the school year is arranged so that students can go out on the land with their families to hunt, fish, and trap during fall and spring.

*Schoolchildren play outside Arctic Bay School on Baffin Island.*

Radio and television programs also help preserve Inuit culture. Some shows are broadcast in the Inuktitut language. One northern television network is run entirely by Aboriginal people.

Inuit are famous all over the world for their superb sculptures. In fact, the largest carving ever made stands in the lobby of a bank in Toronto, Ontario, in southern Canada. This sculpture was carved by a team of Inuit and non-Inuit working together on a lonely marble beach near Cape Dorset on Baffin Island. The carving stands as an example of how Native and non-Native people can learn from one another—and build not only a sculpture but a new territory and government.

*Lighting a* kudlik *(traditional soapstone lamp) is a symbol of passing on knowledge from one generation to the next or from one culture to another.*

# Famous People from Nunavut

**1** **Susan Aglukark** (born 1967), from Arviat, sings about modern Inuit life. In 1994 she was named the top new star at the Canadian Country Music Awards. *Arctic Rose* and *This Child* are her best-known albums.

**2** **John Amagoalik** (born 1947) grew up in Resolute. He has been called the Father of Nunavut for his efforts to create a separate territory for Inuit. In 1993 Amagoalik was chosen to chair the Nunavut Implementation Commission, which is helping to plan the new territory's government.

**3** **Roald Amundsen** (1872–1928), a Norwegian explorer, was the first to sail the Northwest Passage, a water route from Europe to Asia through the Arctic. He spent two winters with the Netsilik Inuit at a place in Nunavut he named Gjoa Haven, after his ship. While there, he studied the Native lifestyle and learned Native survival techniques. Amundsen wrote several books about his explorations.

**4** **Jack Anawak** (born 1950) grew up near Repulse Bay. He is an excellent hunter and businessperson and is also a politician who is active in several Inuit organizations. In 1988 Anawak was elected to serve as the representative from the Eastern Arctic in Canada's House of Commons.

**5** **Kenojuak Ashevak** (born 1927) is a world-famous artist. In 1967 she became the first Native person to receive the Order of Canada, one of the nation's highest awards for achievement. Her drawing *The Enchanted Owl* was reproduced in 1970 as a stamp to mark the 100th anniversary of the Northwest Territories. She lives in Cape Dorset.

**6** **Tagak Curley** (born 1944) spent his early years on the land before his family was moved by the Canadian government to Coral Harbour. In 1971 Curley founded the Inuit Tapirisat of Canada, an Inuit cultural and political organization. He has also worked as a businessperson, was the director of the Inuit Cultural Institute in Rankin Inlet, and was elected to the legislative assembly and the cabinet of the government of the Northwest Territories.

**Edna Elias** (born 1956) has spent her life helping Inuit women. Born at a traditional hunting camp near Cambridge Bay, Elias has been a teacher, an author, and the director of a Native language bureau. In the 1980s, she served as the first female mayor of Coppermine.

**8** **Ann Meekitjuk Hanson** (born 1946) works as a radio broadcaster, writer, interpreter, and member of various science, education, and health boards. Born in a camp near Lake Harbour, she went on to serve as deputy commissioner of the Northwest Territories from 1987 to 1991.

**9** **Kenn Harper** (born 1945) is a teacher, businessperson, historian, and author from Iqaluit. His works include *Give Me My Father's Body* and two books about the Inuktitut language. In 1993 Harper was selected to serve as a member of the Nunavut Implementation Commission.

**10** **James Houston** (born 1921) is an artist, author, and filmmaker. Born in Toronto, Ontario, Houston moved in 1948 to Cape Dorset, where he lived for many years. There he taught Inuit artists several ways to make prints of their drawings and helped publicize Inuit art to the rest of the world. His most famous book and film is *White Dawn*.

■ **Michael Kusugak** (born 1948) didn't think of becoming an author until he met popular children's writer Robert Munsch. Together they wrote *A Promise Is a Promise,* and since then Kusugak has written several more children's books, including the award-winning *Northern Lights: The Soccer Trails.* Kusugak is from Chesterfield Inlet.

**12** **Willy Laserich** (born 1932), president of Adlair Aviation Ltd. in Cambridge Bay, has been a famous bush pilot since 1954. Over the years, he has flown thousands of missions to rescue lost hunters, take people to the hospital, and transport goods to icebound communities.

**13** **William Lyall** (born 1941), born at Fort Ross, has served as a mayor and a member of the legislative assembly of the Northwest Territories. Since 1981 Lyall has been the president of Arctic Co-operatives Ltd., which represents 41 Inuit co-operatives. In 1993 he was appointed to the Nunavut Implementation Commission.

**14** **Helen Mamayaok Maksagak** (born 1931) was appointed commissioner of the Northwest Territories in 1995. She is respected for the work she has done with her church, the police, and social service organizations. Maksagak lives in Cambridge Bay.

**15** **Guy Mary-Rousselière** (1913–1994) was a Catholic missionary from France who spent 55 years in the north, mostly around Pond Inlet. He was also an archaeologist, photographer, filmmaker, and the editor of *Eskimo* magazine.

■ **Abe Okpik** (born 1929) has worked as a teacher, counselor, and politician. He is best known for Project Surname, a program to replace Inuit identification numbers with surnames (family names). Okpik was awarded the Order of Canada in 1976 for this effort. He is from Kipnik.

**17 Jessie Oonark** (1906–1985) was an artist from Baker Lake. Her best-known piece is a print called *Giver of Life*. The Jessie Oonark Centre in Baker Lake is named for her.

**18 Peter Pitseolak** (1902–1973) was an author and the first Inuit to become a professional photographer. He took his first photo for a white man who was afraid to approach a polar bear. Pitseolak's autobiography and history of traditional camp life on Baffin Island is called *People from Our Side*.

**19 Knud Rasmussen** (1879–1933) was a Danish explorer, writer, and filmmaker born in Greenland. He traveled frequently across Greenland and the North American Arctic to study Inuit lifeways. In *Across Arctic America* and other books, Rasmussen described his many journeys.

**20 Nick Sikkuark** (born 1943), once a priest and carpenter, has spent more than 20 years as an internationally known sculptor, drawer, and painter. A resident of Pelly Bay, Sikkuark often combines materials such as soapstone, whalebone, caribou antlers, and fur in the same carving.

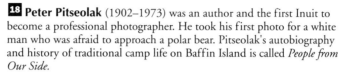

**21 Vilhjalmur Stefansson** (1879–1962), a geographer and lecturer born in Manitoba, spent 12 years in the Canadian Arctic exploring, mapping, and studying Inuit lifeways. His two most famous books are *My Life with the Eskimo* and *Friendly Arctic*.

**22 Charlie Ugyuk** (born 1931), a resident of Taloyoak, is best known for his large soapstone carvings of falcons, polar bears, and demons, as well as for his miniature ivory dog teams and unusual whalebone pieces. His brothers, Judas Ullulaq and Nelson Takkiruq, are also world-famous carvers.

**67**

# Fast Facts

## Territorial Highlights

**Landmarks:** Auyuittuq National Park on Baffin Island, Ellesmere Island National Park, North Baffin National Park, Kekerten Historic Park near Pangnirtung, Qaummaarviit Historic Park near Iqaluit, Katannilik Territorial Park on Baffin Island, Beechey Island, Bathurst Inlet Lodge, Sila Lodge on Wager Bay, Angmarlik Visitors' Centre in Pangnirtung, Northwest Passage Historic Park in Gjoa Haven, Tunooniq Theatre in Pond Inlet, Coman Arctic Gallery in Iqaluit, West Baffin Eskimo Co-operative in Cape Dorset, Jessie Oonark Centre in Baker Lake, Baker Lake Inuit Camp near Baker Lake

**Annual events:** Toonik Tyme in Iqaluit (April), Northern Games in regional centers (July or August), Arctic Winter Games held every other year at various Arctic sites (March), Umingmak Frolics in Cambridge Bay and other communities (April and May), Midnight Sun Marathon in Nanisivik (June), Christmas and spring festivals in all communities

## Population

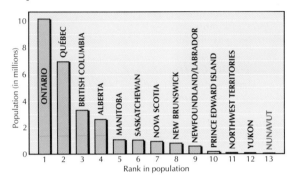

**Population\*:** 24,730
**Rank in population, nationwide:** 13th
**Population density:** 2.9 people per 100 sq mi (1.1 per 100 sq km)
**Capital:** to be decided
**Major communities (and populations\*):** Iqaluit (4,220), Rankin Inlet (2,058), Arviat (1,559), Baker Lake (1,385), Cambridge Bay (1,351), Pangnirtung (1,243), Kugluktuk (1,201)
**Major ethnic groups\*:** Inuit, 80 percent; non-Native, 20 percent
**Official languages:** Inuktitut, English, French

**\*1996 census**

## Endangered, Threatened, and Vulnerable Species

**Mammals:** Peary caribou, bowhead whale, beluga whale, wolverine, grizzly bear, polar bear
**Birds:** Eskimo curlew, tundra peregrine falcon, ivory gull, Ross's gull, short-eared owl
**Fish:** Bering wolffish

## Geographic Highlights

**Area (land/water):** 818,898 sq mi (2,120,948 sq km)
**Rank in area, nationwide:** 1st
**Highest point:** Mount Barbeau (8,583 ft/2,616 m)
**Major rivers:** Coppermine, Hood, Burnside, Back, Thelon, Kazan

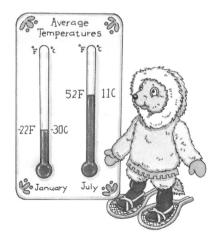

## Economy

**Percentage of Workers Per Job Sector**

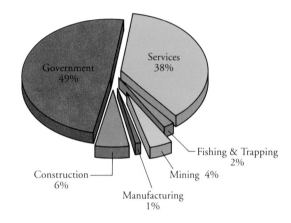

Government 49%
Services 38%
Fishing & Trapping 2%
Mining 4%
Manufacturing 1%
Construction 6%

**Natural resources:** lead, zinc, gold, oil, natural gas, diamonds
**Manufactured goods:** food products (packaged fish and meat), doors, windows

## Energy

**Electric power:** diesel (100 percent)

**69**

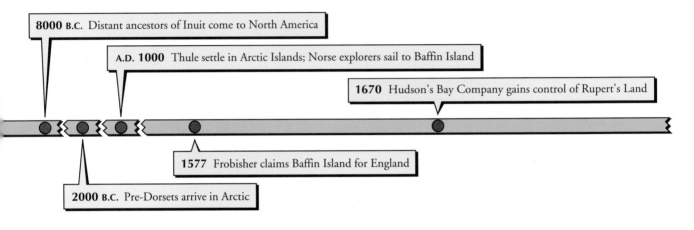

**8000 B.C.** Distant ancestors of Inuit come to North America

**A.D. 1000** Thule settle in Arctic Islands; Norse explorers sail to Baffin Island

**1670** Hudson's Bay Company gains control of Rupert's Land

**1577** Frobisher claims Baffin Island for England

**2000 B.C.** Pre-Dorsets arrive in Arctic

## *Territorial Government*

**Government structure:** Nunavut will have a public government in which all Inuit and non-Inuit can take part. Government institutions will take into account Inuit cultural traditions. The new government will have powers equivalent to those of existing territorial governments. The main governing bodies will be an elected legislative assembly, a cabinet, and a territorial court.

**Capital:** Nunavut is divided into three regions—Qikiqtaaluk (or Baffin) headquartered in Iqaluit, Kivalliq (or Keewatin) based in Rankin Inlet, and Kitikmeot based in Cambridge Bay. One of these three regional headquarters will most likely be chosen as the capital of the territory of Nunavut.

**Voting age:** 16

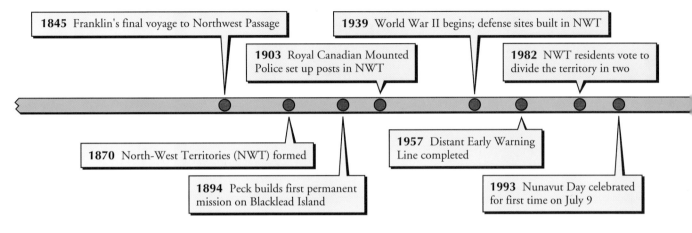

**1845** Franklin's final voyage to Northwest Passage

**1903** Royal Canadian Mounted Police set up posts in NWT

**1939** World War II begins; defense sites built in NWT

**1982** NWT residents vote to divide the territory in two

**1870** North-West Territories (NWT) formed

**1894** Peck builds first permanent mission on Blacklead Island

**1957** Distant Early Warning Line completed

**1993** Nunavut Day celebrated for first time on July 9

## Federal Government

**Capital:** Ottawa
**Head of state:** British Crown, represented by the governor general
**Head of government:** prime minister
**Cabinet:** ministers appointed by the prime minister
**Parliament:** Senate—104 members appointed by the governor general; House of Commons—295 members elected by the people
**Nunavut representation in parliament:** one senator; one house member
**Voting age:** 18

## Government Services

To help pay the people who work for Nunavut's government, residents pay taxes on money they earn and on many of the items they buy. The services run by the territorial government help people in Nunavut meet their needs. The government pays for medical care, for education, for road building and repairs, and for facilities such as libraries and parks. In addition, the government has funds to help people who are disabled, elderly, or poor.

# Glossary

**colony**   A territory ruled by a country some distance away.

**desert**   An area of land that receives only about 10 inches (25 cm) or less of rain or snow a year. Some deserts are mountainous. Others are expanses of rock, sand, or salt flats.

**esker**   A long, narrow ridge or mound of sand and gravel deposited by a stream flowing underneath or in a glacier. When the ice melts, the sand and gravel are left behind.

**glacier**   A huge mass of ice that moves slowly over land. Ice caps and valley glaciers are the two main types of glaciers. Ice caps are very thick, slow-moving glaciers that cover large areas of a continent. Valley glaciers begin on mountains, flow downhill, and often follow paths originally formed by rivers.

**ice age**   A period when ice caps cover large regions of the earth. The term *Ice Age* usually refers to the most recent one, called the Pleistocene, which began almost 2 million years ago and ended about 10,000 years ago.

**missionary**   A person sent out by a religious group to spread its beliefs to other people.

**permafrost**   Ground that remains permanently frozen. A shallow layer of surface soil may thaw during the summer, but the ground below does not.

**precipitation**   Rain, snow, and other forms of moisture that fall to earth.

**swamp**   A wetland permanently soaked with water. In the Arctic, a plant called sphagnum moss is often the main form of vegetation in a swamp.

**tundra** A treeless plain found in Arctic and subarctic regions. The ground beneath the top layer of soil is permanently frozen, but the topsoil thaws for a short period each summer, allowing mosses, lichens, and dwarf shrubs to grow.

## Pronunciation Guide

**Auyuittuq** (ah-yoo-WEE-took)

**Barbeau, Mount** (bahr-BOH)

**Ellesmere** (EHLZ-meer)

**Grise Fiord** (GREES fee-OHRD)

**Inuit** (EE-noo-eet)

**Inuktitut** (ee-NOOK-tih-toot)

**Iqaluit** (ee-KAH-loo-eet)

**Nettilling** (NEHT-uh-ling)

**Nunavut** (NU-nah-voot)

**Pangnirtung** (pang-NYU-tung)

**Thelon** (THEE-lahn)

**Thule** (TOO-lee)

**Tunooniq** (too-NOO-nihk)

**Umingmaktok** (oo-ming-MUHK-tohk)

# Index

# *About the Author*

Lyn Hancock, originally from Australia, has lived in and traveled throughout the Canadian North since 1972. She started her career as an elementary and high-school teacher and is now an award-winning photographer, lecturer, and writer whose books include *There's a Seal in My Sleeping Bag,* and *Yukon,* a Lerner "Hello Canada" title. Ms. Hancock lives in Lantzville, British Columbia.

# *Acknowledgments*

Laura Westlund, pp. 1, 3, 68–71; © Lyn Hancock, pp. 2, 8, 12, 13, 15, 18 (top right), 19, 21 (right and bottom), 25, 40, 42, 44, 44–45, 46 (right), 47, 49, 50 (bottom), 53, 55, 56, 57, 58, 59, 60, 61 (right), 63, 64 (top left), 73, 75, 76; J. F. Bergeron/Travel Arctic, GNWT, pp. 7, 45 (top), 50 (left) 54; Travel Arctic, GNWT, pp. 9, 14, 18, 18 (center left), 45 (bottom); Don Worrall/Travel Arctic, GNWT, pp. 16, 50–51; Dave Monteith/Travel Arctic, GNWT, p. 62; Terry Boles, pp. 6, 10, 48, 69 (bottom left); David Dvorak, Jr., pp. 8 (inset), 17, 20–21; Mapping Specialists Ltd., pp. 10, 11, 48; Ned Therrien, pp. 18 (bottom left), 46 (left), 54 (inset); John Edward Hayashida, pp. 18 (top left), 21 (center); Canadian Museum of Civilization, CMC No. 78–6591, p. 22; West Baffin Eskimo Co-operative Ltd., Cape Dorset, NWT: Soroseelutu Ashoona, *Woman of the Sea,* 1976, p. 23, Kenojuak Ashevak, hand-colored lithograph, *Nunavut,* 1992, p. 43; National Archives of Canada: Neg. Nos. PA129874, p. 26 (left), C3946, p. 27, C8160, pp. 30–31, PA100771, p. 35, PA129942, p. 37 (bottom), PA146647, p. 38, PA129879, p. 39, PA179281, p. 67 (center left), C86406, p. 67 (bottom right); Canadian Museum of Contemporary Photography, p. 26 (right); Metropolitan Toronto Reference Library, pp. 28–29; Dr. Owen Beattie, p. 29 (inset); J. H. A. Wilmot/Hudson's Bay Co. Archives, Provincial Archives of Manitoba, p. 32; Ataguttaaluk School, Igloolik, Canada, p. 33; Dept. of Rare Books and Special Collections, Univ. of Michigan Library, p. 34; Canadian Forces, p. 37 (top); Nunavut Tunngavik Inc., pp. 41, 65 (top); Leena Evic-Twerdin/Nunavut Tunngavik Inc., p. 61 (left); Bill McConkey/Joamie School, p. 52; Library of Congress, pp. 64 (top right), 67 (top right); Terry Pearce/Nunavut Implementation Commission, pp. 64 (center), 65 (bottom left), 66 (center left); Jack Anawak's Office, p. 64 (bottom left); Inuit Art Section, pp. 64 (bottom right), 67 (center right by Larry Ostrum, bottom left by Jeanne L. Pattison); Tessa MacIntosh/Office of the Commissioner of the NWT, pp. 65 (center), 66 (center right); WATT/NWT Archives, p. 65 (bottom right); Joann Laserich, p. 66 (top); Richard Harrington, National Archives of Canada, p.66 (bottom); McCord Museum of Canadian History, Notman Photographic Archives, p. 67 (top left).